WELCOME

To

_____

From

_____

Date

_____

to the CABIN

A smell of men's sweat seemed to permeate the summer air of Fairchilds until you got inside the cemetery. Here sweet dusty honeysuckle—for the vines were pinkish-white with dust, like icing decorations on a cake, each leaf and tendril burdened—perfumed a gentler air, along with the smell of cut-flower stems that had been in glass jars since some Sunday, and the old-summer smell of the big cedars. Mockingbirds sang brightly in the branches, and Fred, a big bird dog, trotted through on the path, taking the short cut to the icehouse where he belonged. Rosebushes thick and solid as little Indian mounds were set here and there with their perennial worn little birdnests like a kind of bloom.

—Delta Wedding

The old cemetery is there still, like a roof of marble and moss overhanging the town and about to tip into it.

—"Some Notes on River Country"

. . . the houses merge into a shaggy fringe at the foot of the bluff. It is like a town some avenging angel has flown over, taking up every second or third house and leaving only this. There are more churches than houses now; the edge of town is marked by a little wooden Catholic church tiny as a matchbox, with twin steeples carved like icing, over a stile in a flowery pasture.

—"Some Notes on River Country"

. . . down below, Mr. John David's boy opens the wrought-iron gate to the churchyard of the rose-red church, and you go up the worn, concave steps. The door is never locked, the old silver knob is always the heat of the hand. It is a church, upon whose calm interior nothing seems to press from the outer world, which, though calm itself here, is still "outer." (Even cannonballs were stopped by its strong walls, and are in them yet.) It is the kind of little church in which you might instinctively say prayers for your friends.

—"Some Notes on River Country"

The grave hole, up close, smelled like the iron shovel that had dug it and the wet ropes that would harness the coffin down into it. As though thirsty and greedy enough to take anything, it had swallowed all the rain it had received and waited slick and bright.

—Losing Battles

INDEX OF PHOTOGRAPHS

45   Utica: Cemetery monument, woman with wreath. 1935-36

46   Unidentified: Cemetery monument, "Moguin." Post-1936

47   Unidentified: Cemetery monument, woman with hair in bun. Post-1936

48   Jackson's Greenwood Cemetery: Cemetery angel. Post-1936

50   Jackson's Greenwood Cemetery: Cemetery angel. 1935-36

51   Unidentified: Cemetery monument, "Louise Eugenia." Post-1936

52   Brandon: Cemetery angel. Post-1936

53   Crystal Springs: Cemetery monument, "Lily." 1935-36

54   Unidentified: Cemetery angel and cross. Post-1936

55   Brandon: Cemetery monument, woman and cross. Post-1936

56   Unidentified: Cemetery monument, figure kneeling before cross. Post-1936

57   Crystal Springs: Cemetery monument, angel with cross. Post-1936

58   Utica: Untitled. Cemetery monument, "Come Ye Blessed." Post-1936

59   Unidentified: Cemetery monuments. Post-1936

60   Unidentified: Cemetery monument, "Charlie M." Post-1936

61   Unidentified: Cemetery monument, fallen tree. Post-1936

62   Unidentified: Cemetery monument, overturned basket. Post-1936

63   Jackson's Greenwood Cemetery: Cemetery monument, woman with wreath. 1935-36

64   Crystal Springs: Cemetery monument, "Mott." 1935-36

65   Jackson's Greenwood Cemetery: Cemetery monument, dog on grave. Post-1936

66   Jackson's Greenwood Cemetery: Cemetery monument. Post-1936

67   Unidentified: Cemetery monument, dove atop gravestone. Post-1936

68   Port Gibson: Decorative cemetery gate. Post-1936

69   Jackson's Greenwood Cemetery: Cemetery monument, mother and children beneath weeping willow. 1935-36

70   Unidentified: Cemetery monument, arch. Post-1936

71   Unidentified: Cemetery monument, "Miller." Post-1936

72   Utica: Cemetery lamb. Post-1936

73   Unidentified: Cemetery lamb. Post-1936

74   Unidentified: Cemetery monument, "Infant Dau. of J. W. & H. M. Barber." Post-1936

75   Unidentified: Cemetery monument, "Perry W." Post-1936

76   Jackson's Greenwood Cemetery: Cemetery monument, "Onslow Glenmore." Post-1936

77   Vicksburg: Cemetery monument, "John B. Reid, Jr." Post-1936

Library of Congress Cataloging-in-Publication Data

Welty, Eudora, 1909–

Country Churchyards / Eudora Welty.

p. cm.

ISBN 1-57806-235-7 (Cloth : alk. paper)

1. Cemeteries—Mississippi—Pictorial works.

2. Mississippi—History, Local—Pictoral works. 1. Title.

F342.W44 2000

976.2—dc21   99–052960

British Library Cataloging-in-Publication Data available

I'D RATHER BE
Lost at the Cabin

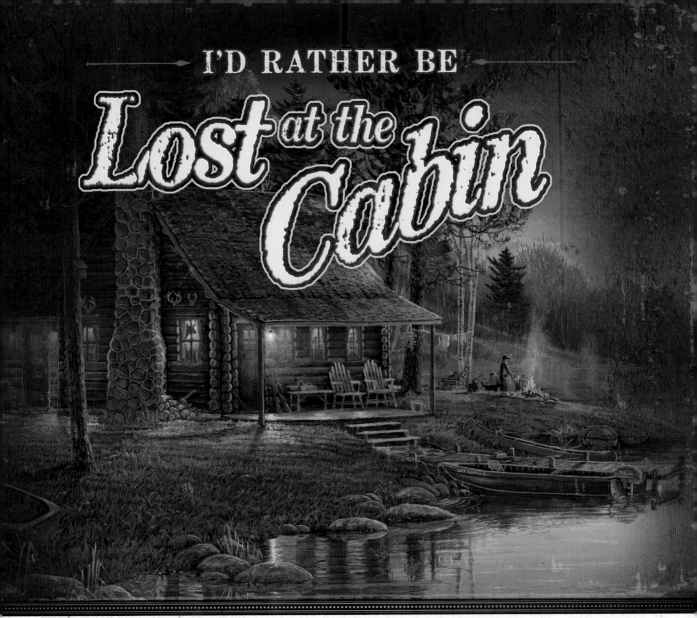

Paintings by **Sam Timm**, **Rosemary Millette**, *and* **Persis Clayton Weirs**

HARVEST HOUSE PUBLISHERS
EUGENE, OREGON

I'd Rather Be Lost at the Cabin

Artwork copyright© by Wild Wing Artists. Courtesy of Wild Wings, LLC, Lake City, Minnesota 55041. www.wildwings.com

Published by Harvest House Publishers
Eugene, Oregon 97402
www.harvesthousepublishers.com

ISBN 978-0-7369-5325-2

Design and production by Left Coast Design, Portland, Oregon

Printed in China

13 14 15 16 17 18 19 20 21 / LP / 10 9 8 7 6 5 4 3 2 1

*Nothing is worth
more than this day.*

JOHANN WOLFGANG VON GOETHE

How strange that Nature does not
knock, and yet does not intrude!

EMILY DICKINSON

He sendeth sun, he sendeth shower,
Alike they're needful for the flower;
And joys and tears alike are sent
To give the soul fit nourishment.

SARAH FLOWER ADAMS

And this, our life, exempt from public
haunt, finds tongues in trees, books
in the running brooks, sermons in
stones, and good in everything.

WILLIAM SHAKESPEARE

You will find something far greater
in the woods than you will find in books.
Stones and trees will teach that which
you will never learn from masters.

SAINT BERNARD

Luck affects everything. Let your hook always be cast; in the stream where you least expect it, there will be a fish.

Ovid

There is another sky,
Ever serene and fair,
And there is another sunshine,
Though it be darkness there;
Never mind faded forests, Austin,
Never mind silent fields–
Here is a little forest,
Whose leaf is ever green;
Here is a brighter garden,
Where not a frost has been;
In its unfading flowers
I hear the bright bee hum:
Prithee, my brother,
Into my garden come!

EMILY DICKINSON

Any man that walks the mead
In bud, or blade, or bloom, may find
According as his humors lead,
A meaning suited to his mind.

ALFRED TENNYSON

Smooth runs the water where the brook is deep.

WILLIAM SHAKESPEARE

As the deer pants for streams of water, so my soul pants for you, my God. My soul thirsts for God, for the living God.

THE BOOK OF PSALMS

My profession is always to be alert, to find God in nature, to know God's lurking places, to attend to all the oratorios and the operas in nature.

HENRY DAVID THOREAU

If you truly love Nature, you will find beauty everywhere.

VINCENT VAN GOGH

Water is
the driver
of Nature.

LEONARDO
DA VINCI

Nature has some perfections,
to show that she is the image of
God; and some defects, to show
that she is only His image.

BLAISE PASCAL

Adopt the pace of Nature: her secret is patience.

RALPH WALDO EMERSON

You must not know too much, or be too
precise or scientific about birds and trees and
flowers and water-craft; a certain free margin and
even vagueness—perhaps ignorance, credulity—
helps your enjoyment of these things.

WALT WHITMAN

*There is
no greatness
where there is
not simplicity.*

LEO TOLSTOY

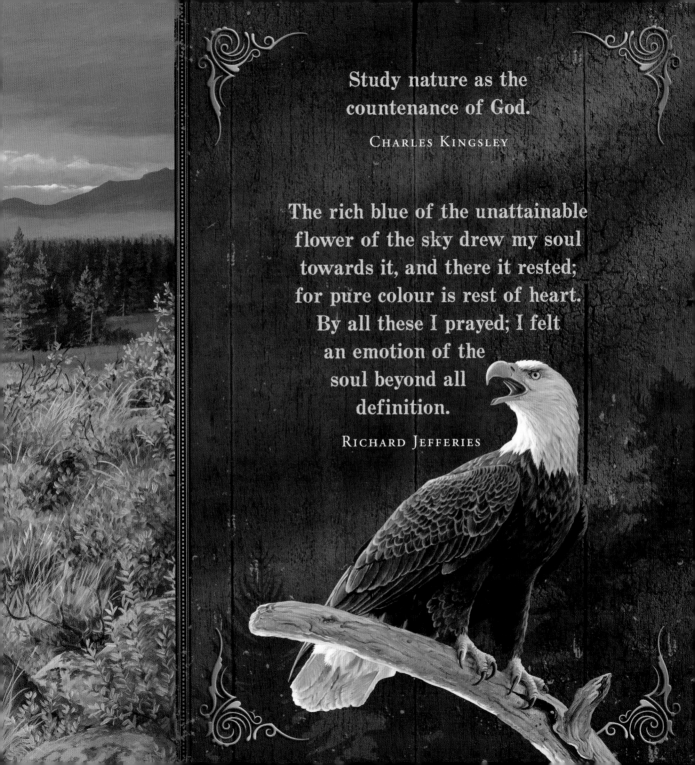

Study nature as the
countenance of God.

CHARLES KINGSLEY

The rich blue of the unattainable
flower of the sky drew my soul
towards it, and there it rested;
for pure colour is rest of heart.
By all these I prayed; I felt
an emotion of the
soul beyond all
definition.

RICHARD JEFFERIES

My heart is awed within me when I think
Of the great miracle that still goes on,
In silence, round me—the perpetual work
Of thy creation, finished, yet renewed
Forever. Written on thy works I read
The lesson of thy own eternity.

WILLIAM CULLEN BRYANT

Beautiful landscape! I could look
   on thee
For hours,—unmindful of the storm
   and strife,
And mingled murmurs of
   tumultuous life.
Here, all is still as fair—the stream,
   the tree,
The wood, the sunshine on the bank,
   no tear—
No thought of Time's swift wing,
   or closing night,
Which comes to steal away the
   long sweet light,—
No sighs of sad humanity, are here.

WILLIAM LISLE BOWLES
from "On a Beautiful Landscape"

God writes the gospel not in
the Bible alone, but on trees and
flowers and clouds and stars.

MARTIN LUTHER

Truths are first clouds; then rain, then harvest and food.

HENRY
WARD BEECHER

I wist not what to wish, yet sure thought I,
If so much excellence abide below;
How excellent is he that dwells on high?
Whose power and beauty by his works we know.
Sure he is goodness, wisdom, glory, light,
That hath this under world so richly dight.
More Heaven than Earth was here,
no winter and no night.

ANNE BRADSTREET

*A lake
carries you
into recesses
of feeling
otherwise
impenetrable.*

WILLIAM
WORDSWORTH

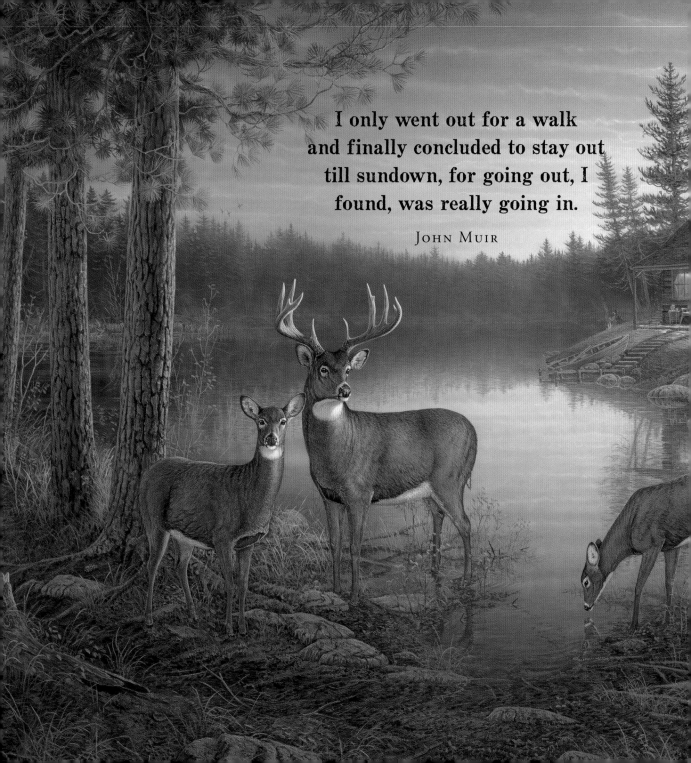

I only went out for a walk
and finally concluded to stay out
till sundown, for going out, I
found, was really going in.

JOHN MUIR

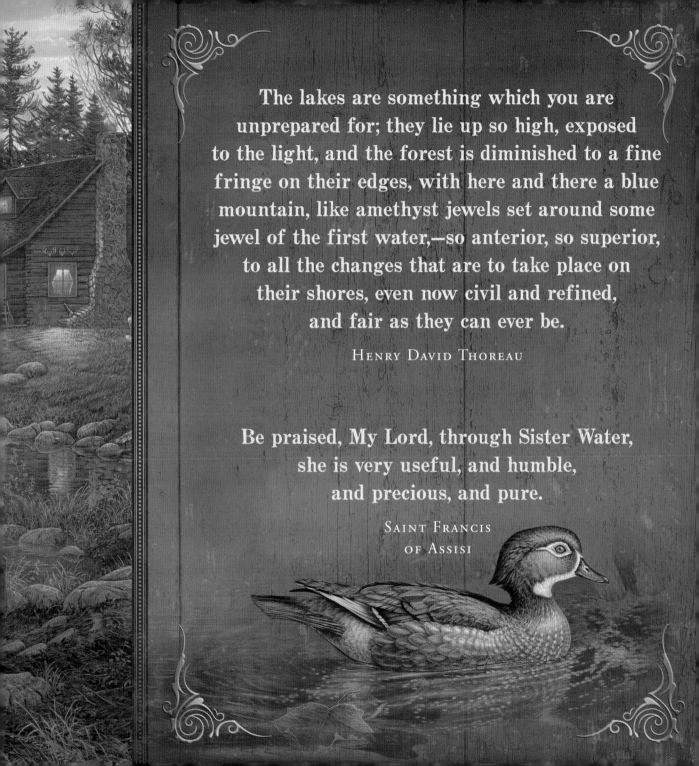

The lakes are something which you are unprepared for; they lie up so high, exposed to the light, and the forest is diminished to a fine fringe on their edges, with here and there a blue mountain, like amethyst jewels set around some jewel of the first water,—so anterior, so superior, to all the changes that are to take place on their shores, even now civil and refined, and fair as they can ever be.

HENRY DAVID THOREAU

Be praised, My Lord, through Sister Water, she is very useful, and humble, and precious, and pure.

SAINT FRANCIS
OF ASSISI

We do not see
nature with our
eyes, but with our
understandings
and our hearts.

WILLIAM HAZLITT

Fair tree! for thy delightful Shade
'Tis just that some Return be made;
Sure, some Return is due from me
To thy cool Shadows, and to thee.

ANNE KINGSMILL FINCH
from "The Tree"

Sit in reverie, and watch
The changing color of the waves
    that break
Upon the idle seashore of the mind.

HENRY WADSWORTH LONGFELLOW

The serene, silent beauty of a
holy life is the most powerful
influence in the world, next to
the might of the Spirit of God.

BLAISE PASCAL

Boldly and wisely in
that light thou hast—
There is a hand above
will help thee on.

PHILIP JAMES BAILEY

The sun upon the lake is low,
The wild birds hush their song.

SIR WALTER SCOTT

To find the universal elements enough;
to find the air and the water exhilarating;
to be refreshed by a morning walk or an evening
saunter; to find a quest of wild berries more
satisfying than a gift of tropic fruit; to be
thrilled by the stars at night; to be elated
over a bird's nest, or over a wildflower
in spring—these are some of the
rewards of the simple life.

JOHN BURROUGHS

Depend upon it, God's work done in God's way will never lack God's supplies.

J. HUDSON TAYLOR

Who publishes
the sheet-music
of the winds
or the music of
water written
in river-lines?

JOHN MUIR

This is the meeting place where God
has set his bounds. Here is enough, at last,
for eye and thought, restful and satisfying and
illimitable. Here rest is sweet, and the picture
of it goes with us on our homeward way,
more lasting in memory than the sunset
on the meadows or the lingering
light across the silent stream.

Isaac Ogden Rankin

I looked in the brook and saw a face—
Heigh-ho, but a child was I!
There were rushes and willows in that place,
And they clutched at the brook as the brook ran by;
And the brook it ran its own sweet way,
As a child doth run in heedless play,
And as it ran I heard it say:
"Hasten with me
To the roistering sea
That is wroth with the flame of the morning sky!"

EUGENE FIELD, from "The Brook"

Sweet bird, that sing'st away the early hours
Of winters past or coming, void of care,
Well pleased with delights which present are,
(Fair seasons, budding sprays, sweet-smelling flowers)
To rocks, to springs, to rills, from leafy bowers
Thou thy Creator's goodness dost declare.

WILLIAM DRUMMOND, from "To the Nightingale"

Any one thing in the creation
is sufficient to demonstrate
a Providence to a humble
and grateful mind.

EPICTETUS

I go to nature to be soothed
and healed, and to have my
senses put in order.

JOHN BURROUGHS

Do not hover always on the surface of things, nor take up suddenly with mere appearances; but penetrate into the depth of matters, as far as your time and circumstances allow. ISAAC WATTS

The Lord my pasture
    shall prepare,
And feed me with a
    shepherd's care
His presence shall my
    wants supply,
And guard me with a
    watchful eye.

JOSEPH ADDISON

Love all God's creation,
both the whole and every
grain of sand. Love every
leaf, every ray of light.
Love the animals, love the
plants, love each separate
thing. If thou love each
thing thou wilt perceive
the mystery of God in all.

FYODOR DOSTOEVSKY

Peace like the river's gentle flow,
Peace like the morning's silent glow,
From day to day, in love supplied,
An endless and unebbing tide.

HORATIUS BONAR

Just as there comes a warm
sunbeam into every cottage window,
so comes a love-beam of God's care
and pity, for every separate need.

NATHANIEL HAWTHORNE

I hear lake water lapping with
low sounds by the shore. . .
I hear it in the deep heart's core.

WILLIAM BUTLER YEATS

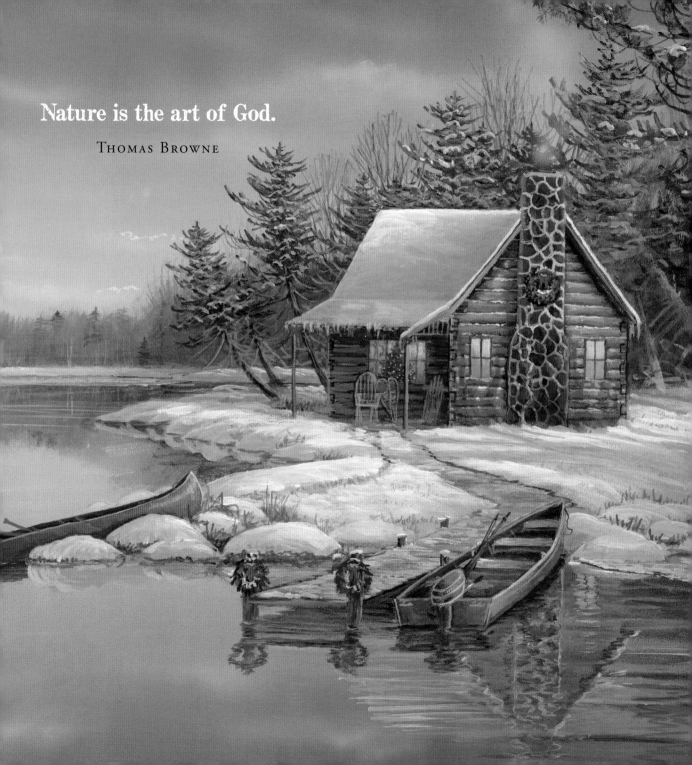

Nature is the art of God.

THOMAS BROWNE

The richness I achieve comes from
Nature, the source of my inspiration.

CLAUDE MONET

Nature is man's teacher. She unfolds
her treasures to his search, unseals his eye,
illumes his mind, and purifies his heart; an
influence breathes from all the sights
and sounds of her existence.

ALFRED BILLINGS STREET

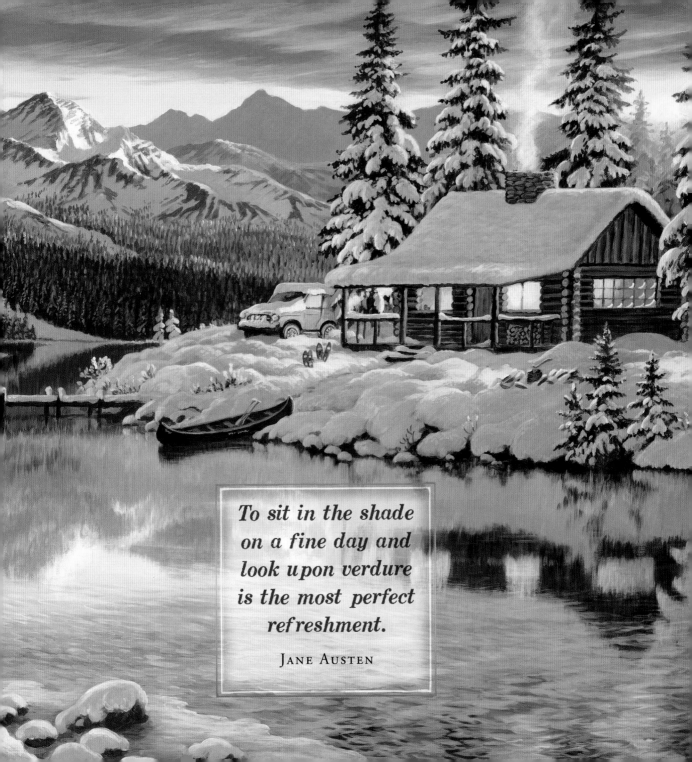

To sit in the shade
on a fine day and
look upon verdure
is the most perfect
refreshment.

JANE AUSTEN

For stars that pierce
the somber dark,
For morn, awaking
with the lark,
For life new-stirring
'neath the bark,—

For sunshine and the
blessed rain,
For budding grove and
blossoming lane,
For the sweet silence
of the plain,—

For bounty springing
from the sod,
For every step by
beauty trod,—
For each dear gift of
joy, thank God!

FLORENCE EARLE COATES

Away up in the very heart of Maine there is a mighty lake among the mountains. . . You find that you have plunged into a new world—a world that has nothing in common with the world that you live in; a world of wild, solemn, desolate grandeur, a world of space and silence; a world that oppresses your soul—and charms you irresistibly. And after you have once "come out" of that world, there will be times, to the day of your death, when you will be homesick for it, and will long with a childlike longing to go back to it.

HENRY CUYLER BUNNER

A thing of beauty is a joy forever.

JOHN KEATS

Nature I'll court in her sequester'd haunts,
By mountain, meadow, streamlet, grove or cell;
Where the pois'd lark his evening ditty chaunts,
And health, and peace, and contemplation dwell.

Tobias Smollett

There is nothing that God hath established in a
constant course of nature, and which therefore is done
every day, but would seem a Miracle, and exercise
our admiration, if it were done but once.

John Donne

True silence is the rest of the mind; and is to the spirit what sleep is to the body, nourishment and refreshment.

WILLIAM PENN

There is one piece of advice, in a life of study, which I think no one will object to; and that is, every now and then to be completely idle—to do nothing at all.

SYDNEY SMITH

In all things of nature
there is something of
the marvelous.

ARISTOTLE

Two things fill me with constantly
increasing admiration and awe, the longer
and more earnestly I reflect on them:
the starry heavens without and
the moral law within.

IMMANUEL KANT

Clouds, lingering yet, extend in solid bars
Through the grey west; and lo!
These waters, steeled
By breezeless air to smoothest polish, yield
A vivid repetition of the stars.

WILLIAM WORDSWORTH

Like two cathedral
  towers these stately
  pines
Uplift their fretted
  summits tipped with
  cones;
The arch beneath them
  is not built with
  stones—
Not Art but Nature
  traced these lovely
  lines,
And carved this graceful
  arabesque of vines.

HENRY WADSWORTH
  LONGFELLOW

from "My Cathedral"